DEDICATION

To Betsy Fontes, for showing me that a friend is always there no matter what.

ACKNOWLEDGMENTS

I gratefully acknowledge the guidance and support of the following individuals who have encouraged growth in all areas of my relationships: To Ellen Ratner, who pointed my way down the road of adult children's issues; to Barbara Kliman, who helped me with couple counseling; and to Bonnie Broe, who has been my support through a recovery replete with learning. Also to Bonnie, I extend my heartfelt appreciation for her reading and encouragement of the draft of this book.

CONTENTS

INTRODUCTION

As adult children, our recovery can be likened to the story of Rip Van Winkle who awakened after many years of sleep to a strange and new world. Many times we may feel the same out-of-touch feeling Rip Van Winkle felt. We may not know quite what to do in the world of adulthood that surrounds us because we may have never been given the tools or had the experiences and feelings in the past that we needed to grow and mature in the present.

To begin recovering, we need to rouse ourselves from the sleep of the past and come to a gradual awakening. This awakening involves a process of awareness, where we learn past messages and experiences may not be the right messages and experiences to apply to the present. In some cases, we need to let go of the negative elements of the past in favor of more positive ones in the present. In other cases, we need to discard many of the old ways of doing things and learn new behaviors.

One such area of learning occurs in forming and maintaining relationships. As a group, adult children have a particularly difficult time interacting with people. People who don't understand or share the same background as an adult child may not comprehend the multitude of difficulties we face in every kind of relationship.

Why do we seem to flounder helplessly in our interactions with others? Why do we run from intimate relationships? Why do we feel inner tension and doubt when others enjoy spending time with us? Why can we rarely experience serenity in a relationship, opting instead to create chaos or crisis? Why do we find it so difficult to express personal desires? Why do we choose to stay in relationships that are painful?

All these dilemmas — and more — can be felt by adult children whenever we interact with others. Many of us find ourselves fumbling our way through present relationships because we relive the relationship behaviors we saw in our dysfunctional past. As a result, our present relationships can't get any better unless we acquire new tools and use them to make changes.

1

This book is designed to offer those tools to the adult child who may be ready to learn the elements involved in healthy relationships. The first part of the book is designed to help us understand unhealthy relationships and why we may keep forming them. The second part of the book discusses the elements we can use to help make our present relationships healthier. The examples used to illustrate both unhealthy and healthy relationship behaviors may seem very familiar. The examples are not intended as real stories but as composites for illustrative purposes.

Identification is a vital component in making changes in our lives. It's important that we can say, "Yes, that sounds like me," or, "My life has been just like that," to help us identify our feelings and behaviors. The reflection and activity sections at the end of each chapter may be helpful in assisting us in our identification process. We may also wish to write our responses in a notebook. If we date our writings, we can reread this book at other times in the future and contribute new responses to our notebook. Our journal can then be used as a valuable tool, not only in our identification process but also as a reflection of positive growth and changes that are certain to be part of our recovery.

Through awareness comes change; through change comes growth. But this process doesn't occur unless we want it to happen. The key word to remember in all our recovery work is *choice*. In recovery, we are given the keys to open various doors to healthy growth and change. It is our choice whether to open the doors or not. As Joseph Epstein said in *Ambition: The Secret Passion:*

> We do not choose to be born. We do not choose our parents. . . . But within all this realm of choicelessness, we do choose how we shall live . . . these choices and decisions are ours to make. We decide. We choose. And as we decide and choose, so are our lives formed.

It is my strong hope you will find tools in this book that will help you build strong and healthy relationships.

PART I

UNDERSTANDING UNHEALTHY RELATIONSHIPS

If you carry your childhood with you,
you never become older.
— Abraham Sutzhever

CHAPTER ONE

Relationships and Adult Children

Many people associate the term *relationship* with love or sexual interactions. Because of that association, *relationship* has the power to evolve into a feared word. Then it begins with a big, bold capital R and symbolizes pain, sadness, and rejection.

For the purposes of this book, *relationship* is defined as our connection with any person who has a reason to be in our lives, including friends, business associates, group affiliations, and social contacts, as well as love or sexual interactions.

What Is a Healthy Relationship?

Whether a relationship lasts a few months or many years, the important question to ask about it is: Is it healthy? That question may be difficult to answer if we don't know what a healthy relationship is. Just because a relationship has lasted for a long time doesn't necessarily mean it's healthy; similarly, a relationship that lasts only a few months isn't necessarily unhealthy.

This book explores the differences between unhealthy and healthy relationships. In Part I, we'll learn how some of our present relationships could have arrived at their current unhealthy state. In Part II, we'll learn how to improve our relationships by work in five specific areas: trust, honesty, individuality, nurturing, and knowledge. We may hear or we may know for ourselves that any relationship requires work, but healthy relationships also require thought. Take the first letter of each of the five elements — Trust, Honesty, Individual-

5

ity, Nurturing, and Knowledge — and they spell THINK. A relationship that doesn't have all five qualities of THINK probably isn't as healthy as it could be.

But before we can begin to do the work to improve the quality of our relationships, we need to explore why we haven't been able to form healthy relationships up to this point in time. As adult children, this inability may have had its basis in the past. Because of that, we need to look back to our childhood and the messages we received to understand why we have difficulties forming healthy relationships as adults.

Who Are Adult Children?

People who grow up in dysfunctional homes and reach adulthood without dealing directly with the effects of such a childhood are called adult children. The dysfunction in the home could have been exhibited in blatant or subtle ways. Dysfunctions include alcohol or other drug addictions, eating disorders, compulsive gambling, sexual or physical disorders, or sexual or physical abuse of a spouse, child, or both. Other dysfunctions include workaholism, mental illness, emotional problems, a history of alcoholism in the family tree, or emotional abuse of a spouse, child, or both. Separations, divorce, adoption, and inconsistent guardianship of children by family members or foster homes may also cause dysfunction in the family.

Messages Carried Into Adulthood

The first relationships we have are with our mothers and fathers. These relationships set the parameters for many of the relationships we form in adulthood. When dysfunction exists in the home, the focus is usually placed on the dysfunction and the parent who exhibits the dysfunction. Attention to other family members becomes secondary to the compulsions or negative behaviors. Some of us would portray it as a frenzied whirlpool of crazy behaviors and abnormal emotions.

Because the emphasis in the home is on the dysfunction, sacrifices are made in relationships. Sometimes people aren't viewed as important; the expression of individual needs and wants is rarely en-

6

couraged. Individuals in the family may be ignored, stirring up feelings of abandonment and rejection.

Oftentimes relationships travel on a roller coaster ride. One minute the child may be important and close to a parent; the next minute the child may be pushed away. Because the messages aren't clear, we may have little or no security or consistency in our relationships. Mixed messages abound in the dysfunctional home, such as:

"I love you. Go away."
"You're important to me. I don't have time for you."
"I want to hear how you feel. Stop crying."
"We'll go away on a trip together. We'll do it some other time."
"You're doing just fine. Why can't you do better?"

Sometimes inconsistencies are expressed verbally. Other times they're expressed in inconsistent behaviors. Parents who say they'll be there and then are not (emotionally as well as physically) may lead us to believe we will be abandoned in other relationships. Parents who express love and then become sexually, physically, or verbally abusive teach us that being loved means being abused. We may then form relationships with people who perpetuate those same behaviors because we've been taught this is how love is expressed. If we've had inconsistent guardianship in childhood, we may have difficulty making a commitment to anyone in adulthood, believing relationships will be temporary. If we've been the responsible one in our childhood home, we may form relationships with people who are insecure and dependent; those people will lean on our overdeveloped sense of responsibility.

In summary, if the relationship we had with our parents was filled with mixed messages, inconsistent behaviors, and unhealthy emotional responses, those messages may comprise the blueprints we use in building relationships as adults.

Keep in mind we will most likely gravitate toward the familiar in all our relationships. We may start to see our parents' behaviors in our boss, co-workers, close friends, spouse, or lover. This may make the

7

relationships extremely difficult for us. That's not unusual! Our past has a powerful influence on our present interactions. But once we understand these influences, we can change them.

The Influences of the Past

As adult children, we may learn to live life with three familiar feelings: fear, doubt, and insecurity. The dysfunctional childhood home plants the seeds for these feelings; years spent in the chaotic, emotionally-starved home nourish these seeds until they sprout and flourish. Over time, the adult child becomes used to these feelings in adult interactions. Their influence is felt in all facets of adult life, particularly in forming relationships.

Fear

Abandonment/Isolation. When we feel fear in our relationships, one of our first reactions may be to isolate. This means avoiding other people. One of the reasons we feel fear is not wanting to be abandoned and left alone as we were in childhood. If we don't form any relationships, we won't be hurt, abandoned, let down, or rejected. We may see isolation as safe and relationships as unsafe.

* * *

Elisabeth had been dating Andy for a few months. She liked him right away and was surprised when he kept asking her out. She enjoyed dating him and developed strong feelings for him.

One night Andy told her he had to go on a business trip for a few days. Elisabeth's chest began to tighten as she listened to him, and she felt like she couldn't breathe. She felt panicky, like a little girl who was going to be left alone for the first time.

She did not let Andy know her tense feelings that evening, but in a short while she may end up doing one of three things. She may start an argument before he leaves on the trip over a petty detail so she feels justified that he's leaving while she's angry at him; not tell Andy anything about her panicky feelings, but decide while he's gone that she really didn't care as much for him as she thought she had — and decide not to see him again; or clutch desperately onto Andy un-

8

til he has to go away, fearful that he'll be going away from her for good.

*   *   *

What Elisabeth is feeling when she hears Andy tell her he's going away for a short while is a past message that relationships mean abandonment. In Elisabeth's painful past, her father left the family when she was six; in adulthood, she never learned that people can separate for a short time. Her fear turned into isolation and prevented her from continuing to form other intimate relationships.

Lack of Control. Fear can also result from not wanting to be out of control. In childhood, life may have been chaotic. The fear that adulthood might also be as unpredictable can result in inflexibility in taking relationship risks. That out-of-control feeling may happen whenever the other person makes personal decisions.

*   *   *

Stephanie made plans a week in advance to go to a movie with Julie Friday night. Thursday night Julie called her to reschedule. She felt she had been burning the candle at both ends all week and decided the best thing for her to do Friday night was take a hot bath and go to bed early. But she told Stephanie Sunday night would be fine.

Even though Stephanie had no plans for Sunday night she said no. After all, she thought, she had made the plans for Friday and they really should stick to that night. She argued with Julie, trying to convince her to get extra sleep Saturday morning so she could still go to the movie on Friday. Julie said no, but added that she would be happy to go to a movie another time. Stephanie said she'd think about it and hung up in a huff.

*   *   *

Feelings of being out of control can also occur if we are asked to spend the night over at another person's house, are a passenger in another person's vehicle, need to go someplace unfamiliar, or do new and different things. This type of fear can restrict us from meeting new people and experiencing new situations. Because of this, we may

9

choose to stay in friendships, jobs, and love relationships that are familiar — even if they're uncomfortable and unhealthy — rather than lose control.

Dependency. Fear can also result from not wanting to be dependent upon others. We may have learned early in life that relying on a dysfunctional parent usually meant disappointment and rejection. Our approach in adulthood, therefore, may be one of strong-willed independence. The message we give to others is we need no one; this becomes quite clear to any co-worker, friend, or lover who wants to assist us or offer us support, nurturing, or love.

*   *   *

Bob woke up one morning to discover his car wasn't running smoothly. He dropped it off at the shop and was informed the car couldn't be fixed until the next week. That meant Bob had no way of getting back and forth to work.

Rather than ask Paul, a co-worker who lived near him, for a ride, Bob priced rental cars. When Paul found out what Bob was doing he said he'd give him all the rides he needed and would let him borrow his car over the weekend if he needed one. Bob felt embarrassed by the attention and refused the help. He ended up spending $200 he couldn't afford on a rental car.

*   *   *

Bob confused asking for help with the fear that he wasn't able to stand on his own two feet and solve his own problems. This fear of dependency kept him from spending time with Paul and perhaps developing a close, on-the-job relationship.

Intimacy. Intimacy may be extremely uncomfortable for us because it may not have been consistent when we were growing up. Closeness may also be foreign to us if feelings were not expressed in our childhood homes. Distance, lack of communication, and little or no emotional expression may be far easier for us to handle. In adulthood, we may learn to push away anyone who gets too close or we may shy away from the bonding that occurs in maturing relationships.

10

Intimacy doesn't have to involve sexual or physical contact. The help Paul offered to Bob was a form of intimacy expressed between friends. Stephanie shut herself off from deepening her level of intimacy with Julie by not empathizing with Julie's desire to take care of herself.

Doubt

Perfectionism. We may have a tendency to see things only in terms of black and white in our relationships: right or wrong, long-term or short-term, or be there for me or forget it. Because of this, we may set incredibly high standards of perfection in our relationships. When we do, we set ourselves up for disappointment because nothing can ever be perfect.

The search for perfect relationships may have started in childhood, when we looked around and said, "I will never, ever live like this after I leave here." We may have left home with dreams of relationships where people never argued and everyone understood each other without saying a word. We may have taken those high standards into each of our adult relationships and, whenever there was a problem, we may have immediately suspected the relationship had gone sour. For us, any relationship that didn't feel comfortable and secure all the time was not worth being in.

* * *

Joe was offered a new position in a different department in the company where he worked. He got along well with Marge, the woman who offered him the job.

For the first few months everything went smoothly. Joe couldn't believe how well he liked the job and how pleasant it was to work for Marge. Then Marge's husband was laid off and she began to come to work in a grumpy mood. Her easy-going nature was replaced with a tense, uptight feeling. Joe's perfect job with a perfect boss changed. Rather than try to understand Marge or ride out her temporarily difficult situation, Joe decided his job had gone sour. He started to look for another job.

11

*   *   *

Perfectionism also gets in the way of sexually intimate relationships. We may feel intense excitement at the start of a new relationship. In our eyes the new person may have much more to offer than our last "imperfect" lover. But after awhile, we may begin to find fault with our new lover. What we need to remember is nothing and nobody will ever be perfect. Every relationship has its ups and downs. But if we're looking for perfection we won't be able to tolerate the natural flow of give and take, closeness and separation, sadness and happiness, and change that occurs in relationships.

Lack of Trust. When we were growing up, our parents might have shown us love and affection one day; the next day they might have shown us pain, rejection, or anger. We never knew what would happen from day to day so we learned not to trust what people did, what they said, or the feelings they showed us. For us, trust really never had a chance to grow.

*   *   *

Veronica is the typical overly responsible adult child. She is chairperson of the town historical commission, president of the garden club, sponsor in a Big Sisters program, and contact for newcomers who move to her town.

One day the mayor presented her with a plaque engraved with the words, "To Veronica, for her outstanding dedication to the town from the appreciative townspeople." She smiled obligingly for the photographer while she shook the mayor's hand, but after they left she looked at the plaque and doubted the mayor really meant to give it to her. She didn't believe the sentiments expressed on her gift and felt there was some other reason that the mayor chose to do what he did.

*   *   *

Where there is no trust, there is doubt. If we cannot trust that feelings shown to us by others are genuine or valid, we won't believe them.

12

High Expectations. Because we may find it difficult to believe the validity of any emotion shown in a relationship, we may fantasize about the way things should be. Veronica might have fantasized that she would be rewarded for her outstanding work, but since the plaque wasn't presented to her in front of an audience she may doubt the validity of the mayor's presentation. "Why wouldn't he present the plaque to me in front of a lot of people?" she might ask. Her answer might be he really didn't want to give it to her and didn't believe she was as hard working as he had said. Once again, doubt has set in.

We might also look at television portrayals of relationships as the norm for family, work, friendship, and love relationships. We might also look at fantasy portrayals of relationships for the way things are supposed to be. The standards for family love may become those shown on "The Brady Bunch." The standards for work-place relationships may be those seen on "The Mary Tyler Moore Show." The standards for friendships may be those portrayed on "Laverne and Shirley." The standards for loving relationships may become those described in romance novels.

Believing in idealized relationships creates a model of perfection that can never be satisfied. Therefore, if someone says, "I love you," we may compare the expression and feeling of this emotion to fiction. This may only set us up for disappointment from what we perceive to be imperfect love.

*   *   *

It was Bonnie's and Charles's second anniversary. All day long Bonnie fantasized about a romantic evening with Charles. She put champagne on ice to chill while she waited for him. When he didn't arrive at exactly 6:30 Bonnie waited impatiently for a few minutes, then changed from her negligee into jeans and an old sweatshirt.

Charles arrived home late after fighting his way through rush hour traffic. He opened his briefcase, gave Bonnie a present, and put his arms around her. But Bonnie pushed him away, threw his present to the floor, and pouted in the bedroom for the rest of the night. Her perfect image of their second anniversary didn't occur and she couldn't accept anything less than that dream.

*   *   *

If we have high expectations from our relationships, we may spend a great deal of time fruitlessly looking for the perfect family, job, friends, and lover without realizing perfection doesn't exist. We may continue to doubt the reality of relationships we do have and may reject healthy relationships.

Insecurity

Low Self-Image. When we feel insecure in a relationship we may be feeling the effects of a low self-image. Self-image is defined as how we view ourselves. Because we may have been brought up in a home that didn't encourage individual growth or reinforce our individual abilities and talents, we grew up believing we were inferior to others. We then may have moved into our adulthood relationships with little confidence in ourselves, virtually no self-love, and a feeling we aren't very likable. This low self-image may make us want to isolate from others, push away people who want to get to know us, and refuse any invitations. It can also prevent a love relationship from deepening.

*   *   *

Bill had been dating Connie for six months. One night Connie gave him a gift. "Why are you giving this to me?" he asked.

"Because I love you," was her reply. Bill felt his insides tighten. No one had told him he was loved when he was growing up; in fact, his mother had told him she had no reason to love him. Bill couldn't understand how Connie could love someone as unlovable as he believed he was. He left that night and didn't call her again.

*   *   *

Addiction to People. Because of our insecure feelings, we may choose to be around people who see us as strong and self-assured to counterbalance our low feelings about ourselves. We might also latch onto the first person who pays attention to us because we've been starved for that kind of expression since childhood. We may cling to this person and spend a great deal of time with him or her, becom-

14

ing dependent on the attention and love that makes us feel better about ourselves.

But if the person leaves we may find ourselves feeling such loss and helplessness that we search frantically for someone new to fill the void. We become addicted to people to provide us with a sense of security and a reason to live.

*   *   *

When Susan was seventeen, she became overly anxious to get involved in an intimate relationship. One night she met Scott in a bar. Scott was older, had a professional job, and lived alone in a cozy cabin in the woods. Within a week Susan had moved into Scott's house.

Susan told Scott how afraid she was to apply for jobs. Scott helped her write her resume, suggested jobs for her to apply for, and drove her to interviews. Susan wouldn't do anything without Scott's guidance and support. But after a few months Scott started telling her to do things on her own. When Susan continued to cling onto Scott, he asked her to leave.

Susan felt devastated and alone. A few weeks later she met another man at a party and began a new relationship.

*   *   *

Overcontrol. Some of us take "hostages" in our relationships. We may have difficulty sharing our friends with others, expecting them to always do things with us or be there for us. We may have difficulty allowing our lover or spouse to spend time away from us. We may hold onto each person with a suffocating bondage, keeping him or her prisoner in the relationship with us. Separation may feed into our feelings of insecurity and validate our belief that we have less worth than others.

*   *   *

Jane and Kimberly were close friends. Since their husbands were also close friends with each other, the two couples often spent time together. One weekend, Jane and her husband decided to have a dinner party for some of their friends. When Jane called Kimberly to tell her about the dinner, Kimberly was angry. She hadn't been contacted initially in the party's planning stages or consulted with on the guest list. "After all," she reasoned to Jane, "I'm your best friend."

A few hours before the dinner, Kimberly told her husband she had important errands to run and they would have to arrive late at the party. Kimberly never phoned. Jane and her guests delayed the meal for two hours, waiting for Kimberly and her husband to arrive.

* * *

Kimberly's insecurity over sharing Jane and their relationship with others led her to commit a subtle form of overcontrol. In Kimberly's eyes she punished Jane for not treating Kimberly as the most important friend in her life.

Blame. Insecurities about ourselves and our ability to maintain healthy relationships can lead to a pattern of blaming other people and situations to excuse our inadequacies and to avoid changing our behavior. We might say to others, "If only I met the right lover, then things would work out okay." We may use that line as a standard to fit all our relationships, saying, "If I only had . . . the right friends . . . the right boss . . . the right people on my committee."

When we do this, we're looking for an escape from the layers of childhood pain and sadness. Using blame as a cover for making changes may lead us to believe that past unhealthy relationship issues can only be resolved in the present if the right person can be found.

We may also blame our past as a way of covering up the difficulties we have in the present to form healthy relationships. Then we might strive to look for the right person who will make all our insecurity-based problems better.

* * *

Sally's standard answer to Bob's persistent, "Is there anything bothering you?" is always, "No." Yet Sally goes through periods of time when she alternates between anger, depression, and sadness. Bob never knows what to do then except to ask if she's all right. "Of course I'm not all right," Sally usually snaps back at him. "If you had to grow up in the home that I did, you'd be like this too."

Bob feels helpless whenever Sally tells him this because he believes their relationship is good. He can't understand why Sally always thinks about her awful childhood rather than her nice home, good relationship, and well-behaved kids.

Summary
The influences and messages we received growing up in a dysfunctional home may have played a significant role in the relationships we formed with others. Fear, doubt, and insecurity may have been carried into interactions with friends, co-workers, and intimate partners.

Reflection
Take some time now to think back on the messages you were given in your childhood about relationships with family and friends. What kind of mixed messages did your parents give you while you were growing up? What did they teach you about relationships? What are some of the beliefs and behaviors you've brought into your current relationships?

Activity
Now it's time to examine your personal reactions to this chapter. Use a notebook to write down thoughts on the following areas:

- fear in your relationships;
- doubt in your relationships;
- insecurity in your relationships.

Ask yourself: Have I felt any or all of these in my relationships? How have I expressed these areas, in indirect or direct ways? How have these areas limited me in my interactions with others?

CHAPTER TWO

Living With Unhealthy Relationships

The Negative Effects

The effects of living life without knowing how to form healthy relationships are far from pleasurable. The stresses and pressures we bring into relationships to begin with are usually compounded by the normal stresses and pressures of the relationship. Without knowing how to communicate, trust, and be open and vulnerable, we may feel confused in our relationships. The struggle for us becomes a guessing game as we try to figure out what we're doing wrong so the relationship can be made right.

The normal ebb and flow of any relationship can build into a tidal wave of emotion for us. Everyday occurrences can be misinterpreted, leading to tensions and rifts that weren't intended to be there. Cancelled plans can mean the loss of a friend's caring. An unreturned telephone call can be another rejection. Criticism from an employer can mean the job must be on the line. A lover's desire for solitude may signal the end of the relationship.

When we become overly sensitive to actions, statements, and expressions in relationships, we react rather than act. Because our relationships become difficult to handle, it may be easier for us to cope by falling into one or more of the following roles.

The Roles Played

Isolator

In our childhood, we may have had difficulty forming relationships with people because of shyness or insecurity around others. As we moved into adulthood, we may have found it increasingly difficult to form relationships. We may have cut ourselves off from all interaction with others.

We may keep work relationships at a superficial level and may make little effort to socialize with others unless it's absolutely necessary. We may be uncomfortable at a party and want to leave early. We may hole up in a room or a house, venturing forth only when necessary. We may feel low-level fear whenever we leave the security of our safe space. Very rarely will we initiate telephone calls or extend invitations to others, and we may receive fewer invitations to go out. Or we reject rather than accept invitations we receive.

As isolating adult children, we may eventually accept and even become comfortable with loneliness. We then may avoid any relationship or potential relationship that might take away the security of this loneliness.

What follows are some of the characteristics of the isolator in childhood and adulthood relationships.

As a child, the isolator

- may have very few friends;
- may seem lost in the dysfunctional home and not form a close relationship with either parent or any sibling;
- may like to play alone, often inventing games and scenarios that involve imaginary friends;
- may not be good at or interested in team sports;
- may have a pet as a constant companion;
- may rarely make waves and may seem to have little or no problems;
- may be a good student, a bookworm, or both;
- may go to movies alone, go for solitary walks, collect stamps, or have other isolating hobbies.

As an adult, the isolator

- may have very few friends;
- may date infrequently if single;
- usually lives alone or may live with another isolator;
- may rarely have any personal or social interactions outside of work or the home;
- may disappear easily in a crowd of people;
- may not like to lead any committee or manage others;
- may prefer jobs that have some degree of solitude;
- may not be very confident in his or her abilities, but may work well independently;
- may rarely be late for appointments or for work;
- may prefer not to create waves and avoid situations where controversies or decisions have to be made;
- may be someone who is very difficult to get to know.

People/Love Addict

In our childhood we may have become dependent on our relationships, disliking our solitude so much that we preferred to be around anyone as long as we weren't alone. We may have discovered that when we were out of the house with our friends we didn't have to deal with the pain, anger, and rejection present in our dysfunctional home. We may have also found that spending time with people who were interested in us felt better than the way we were treated at home. We may have grown into adulthood dependent on having relationships with others.

As adults, we may still choose to spend every available minute with others to avoid solitude, which we still associate with pain, anger, and rejection. Friends, acquaintances, organizational groups, and family members may fill our daily schedule.

We may also be involved in an intimate relationship that takes up a great deal of our time. This relationship may be long-term or it may be a new relationship we began shortly after another ended. Looking back on our intimate relationships, we may discover there were only short periods of time when we weren't involved with someone. We may have been involved in numerous relationships, or we may see we've been involved in long-term relationships we were afraid to terminate because of our fear of being alone.

These traits are characteristic of a people/love addict. We will rarely terminate a friendship or intimate relationship that's unhealthy, painful, or has reached the end of its growth. We cling to the person rather than risk being alone.

When a relationship does end, we often rebound quickly into another. Whether the relationship is with a lover, close friend, coworker, or therapist, we may find it much too painful to be "without." Loss of a relationship, no matter what our feelings for the other person, overwhelms us. Rather than deal with the pain of the loss and then accept it, it is easier for us to replace our loss. We are, in effect, escaping from the pain of the past and the present by losing ourselves in addictive relationships. Without solitude, we will have a difficult time learning who we are and what we want; this makes it difficult to develop and maintain healthy relationships.

What follows is a partial listing of some of the characteristics of the people/love addict in childhood and in adulthood relationships. Many of the childhood characteristics may also be felt in adulthood relationships.

In childhood, the people/love addict

- may seem to have a lot of friends and be always busy;
- may enjoy being around other people and dislike being alone;
- may hate being stuck in the house;
- may strive to be liked by others and feel that popularity and image are important;
- may be an average student but may like school mostly for the people and extracurricular activities;
- may date, have sex at an early age, or be promiscuous;
- may be an "idolizer" who puts people up on a pedestal;
- may cling to friends, be possessive of them, and feel jealous when they spend time with others;
- may seem to have few problems or seem to be well-adjusted.

In adulthood, the people/love addict

- may have a busy social calendar;
- may rarely be alone on weekend nights;
- may feel possessive of others and become jealous quite easily;
- may take hostages in relationships;
- may find making a commitment difficult because of the desire not to turn away potential lovers;
- may dislike being alone or working on a solitary job;
- may enjoy being on committees and being a part of a group;
- may make social plans far ahead of time to avoid being alone;
- may dislike cancellations at the last minute.

Manipulator/Controller

In our childhood, we may have observed one parent manipulating and controlling the other. We may have felt the same manipulation and control over ourselves as we were growing up. Either of those situations may have given us the impetus to act out the same behaviors in our relationships.

On the other side of the coin, we may have been brought up feeling certain events and behaviors around us were totally out of control. Because of the discomfort we felt in these unpredictable situations, we may have become manipulating and controlling in order to prevent things in our lives from getting out of control.

Manipulative and controlling behavior leaves very little room for spontaneity or unplanned events in our relationships. They can become structured, rigid, and tense. We may find people shying away from us and not know it's because we are difficult to be around. Our intimate relationships may not last long because we don't give our lover room to grow.

As manipulative and controlling people, we may want others to be who we want them to be, not who they are. Strong, secure, extroverted people may have difficulty with our behaviors, and we often find it easier to form relationships with people who are insecure and allow us to take control.

23

What follows is a partial listing of some of the characteristics of the manipulator/controller in childhood and adulthood relationships. Many of the childhood characteristics may also be felt in adulthood relationships.

In childhood, the manipulator/controller

- may be a leader, team captain, class officer, ringleader in a circle of friends, president of a group, or camp counselor;
- may get good grades or be highly competitive with marks;
- may like team sports, but prefers to be the star;
- may have a "right" way of doing things;
- may usually be the one responsible for the care of the siblings;
- may take care of the dysfunctional parent;
- may strive for perfection and be disappointed when such perfection isn't achieved;
- may like to decide what to do with friends;
- may rarely like to take advice.

In adulthood, the manipulator/controller

- may like to manage, run a business, or hold a position of power at work;
- may like to organize parties and community events;
- may prefer calling the shots in relationships rather than have others make decisions;
- may like to make more money than his or her partner;
- may feel it's not okay for others to cancel plans;
- may not be a good listener;
- may expect all wants or needs to be honored;
- may prefer being around people who can be controlled;
- may like to be the center of attention;
- may be extremely competitive;
- may be easily threatened by others and may feel very insecure.

Dependent/Controlled

The opposite of the manipulator/controller is the person who can be controlled easily and is dependent on others. If we're an isolator we may also find ourselves easily controlled. If we are a people/love addict, we may also feel dependent and controlled because we are affected by the actions of others.

In our childhood, we were probably not the responsible one in the dysfunctional home. Rather, we were usually taken care of by a sibling, parent, or other guardian. Because home was so chaotic and tense, this type of early caretaking may have felt very secure to us. We may carry this dependency on others into adulthood, expecting others to give us the same sense of security we felt when we were younger. This blind faith in others to give us what we need can mean we are easily controlled by others.

It may also mean we are not in touch with our personal needs. We are, in effect, like a weather vane; whichever way the wind is blowing will determine the direction we'll turn. We do not take an active role in our relationships, but will wait to be directed.

What follows is a partial listing of some of the characteristics of the dependent/controlled person in childhood and adulthood relationships. Many of the childhood characteristics may also be felt in adulthood relationships.

In childhood, the dependent/controlled person

- may go along with the crowd;
- may like to be around others but is usually quiet and shy;
- may rarely participate in extracurricular activities;
- may seek a position of responsibility;
- may be very bright but may deliberately try not to show this intelligence;
- may not know how to do laundry, iron, select clothes, cook, and take care of personal hygiene without assistance;
- may rarely do things alone;
- may submit to early sexual encounters but not by choice;
- may be enviable but won't draw attention to self;
- may choose to admire others rather than be admired.

In adulthood, the dependent/controlled

- may have difficulty with compliments or job promotions;
- may prefer to let others take charge;
- may be sexually passive;
- may rarely express a want, need, or preference;
- may not like making choices or decisions;
- may have little direction in life;
- may have qualifications far above the requirements of his or her job;
- may prefer to do things for others in return for protection;
- usually doesn't like to do anything new or different unless he or she is with someone else.

Caretaker/Nurturer

If we grew up taking care of others or seeing others taking care of the dysfunctional parent, our sense of responsibility may have become overdeveloped. If we're a rescuer we may feel a strong need to take care of others while ignoring our own needs. Our happiness may then begin to depend on the state of happiness of those around us, and we may take it upon ourselves to make sure others are fed, clothed, nourished, financially secure, comfortable, healthy, and emotionally supported.

As a rescuer we may also be a manipulator/controller as we take charge of others' lives. We may also be a people/love addict since our dependency on others may include devotion to satisfying their needs.

As a caretaker/nurturer, we may live life believing that others are more important than we are. Rarely do we get to know our own needs, and we may sacrifice our health and happiness while we care for others. While we may feel taking care of others is very self-satisfying, we may be using this unhealthy focus to avoid dealing with our own feelings, needs, and self-nurturing.

We may find our lives filled with relationships, but a closer look may reveal we are doing much of the caretaking, support, and nurturing in those relationships. Rather than growing, our relationships may get bogged down in a quagmire of one-sided giving — with too little given to us.

What follows is a partial list of some of the characteristics of the caretaker/nurturer in childhood and adulthood relationships. Many of the childhood characteristics may also be felt in adulthood relationships.

In childhood, the caretaker/nurturer

- may like to share everything or give coveted items to others;
- may take care of the dysfunctional parent or have a great deal of responsibility around the home;
- may seem easy to get along with;
- may love to please others;
- may try to anticipate needs before they are vocalized by others;
- may strive to get good grades or make great achievements for others;
- may rarely vocalize any dissatisfactions or problems.

In adulthood, the caretaker/nurturer

- may like to buy expensive gifts;
- may choose a career in a helping profession;
- may be a good observer of people and can usually understand how they're feeling;
- may work well with people;
- may be a good listener;
- may seem very devoted to a spouse or lover;
- may put a high value on friendship;
- may go out of his or her way to do something for someone else;
- may like to give parties and entertain.

Fantasizer/Perfectionist

If we're a manipulator/controller, we may also be a fantasizer/perfectionist in our relationships. Our ideal of perfection may be closely linked to our fantasies of what relationships should be. We

27

may struggle to make our relationships perfect through manipulation and control.

If we're an isolator, we may also be a fantasizer/perfectionist. While alone we may dream about how we'd like our relationships to be. We may go to the movies and read novels to escape from real life.

In either case, however, we may see our relationships in terms of what they can be — not what they are. We may see these unhealthy and unhappy relationships as having the potential — somewhere down the road — of changing into happy, healthy ones. We then often find ourselves forming relationships with those who have alcohol or other drug problems, then denying the problem. We may not see the limitations in a friend, co-worker, boss, or partner, choosing to believe he or she can change over time. We may not be able to see incompatibilities in a relationship, choosing instead to believe that if we just hang in there things will work out.

We may end up hanging on to relationships much longer than we should or may place a great deal of faith and hope in the fantasy, rather than the reality, of the people and circumstances of our relationships.

What follows is a partial listing of some of the characteristics of the fantasizer/perfectionist in childhood and adulthood relationships. Many of the childhood characteristics may also be felt in adulthood relationships.

In childhood, the fantasizer/perfectionist

- may isolate or escape into books, television, or movies;
- may be extremely critical of others;
- may have a lot of friends who view him or her as a leader;
- may be obsessive about hobbies;
- may not be able to be objective about his or her own talents and abilities or may not hear criticisms given by others;
- may believe self to be better than others;
- may hero worship movie stars and look for the same qualities in relationships;
- may reject some friendships or intimate relationships if they're not with "the right people."

In adulthood, the fantasizer/perfectionist

- may be judgmental or critical of others;
- may find fault easily with superiors or those in a position of authority;
- may be hard to please;
- may be seen as angry or snobbish;
- may have only short-term relationships with people;
- may isolate or spend a great deal of time doing things in solitude;
- may set incredibly high standards for others to meet.

The Results of Living With Unhealthy Relationships

The effects of unhealthy relationships can have detrimental results over time. Being stuck in any of the familiar but unhealthy roles just discussed means we run the risk of repeating those patterns in all our relationships. We may begin to hear the same personal criticisms and see different relationships end for the same reasons. Over time, we may start to see a pattern.

We may become frustrated with our relationships and seek ways to change them. We may try to psyche ourselves up at the beginning of a relationship and give ourselves a whole list of do's and don'ts we believe will improve our interactions. We may observe someone we admire and try to be more like that person. Or we may buy self-help books and try to pick up some of the positive qualities discussed. Each of these methods may work for a short time, but we often end up repeating our old patterns.

What we're trying to do, in effecting a major behavioral change without the knowledge and the tools, is like trying to build a bookshelf with lots of wood, but no hammer, nails, or saw. In effect, we're trying to get rid of all the bad without realizing we need to revise our behavior.

Failure to change our patterns can lead to deeper entrenchment in those unhealthy roles. Our self-esteem, on shaky ground to begin with, may fall even lower. We may isolate or use food, alcohol, or other drugs to help us cope with our feelings of helplessness. We may change our moral values.

Our low self-worth — combined with other negative messages like self-criticism and hopelessness — can lead to depression, self-abuse, or even suicide attempts in extreme cases.

Hope for recovery rests in a choice: stay in unhealthy relationships and struggle to find health and happiness, or become willing to change old patterns and begin to form healthy relationships.

The choice is similar to seeing a doctor for stress. The doctor can prescribe a pill to ease the symptoms, but that won't make the stress go away. The only way to eliminate it is to eliminate the cause of the stress and learn healthier ways to cope. Likewise, the only way to eliminate the formation of unhealthy relationships is to become aware of what causes them.

Summary

You may always have some negative qualities in your interactions with others, no matter how healthy, happy, and whole you become in your recovery. The roles you may have played thus far in your relationships are deeply ingrained and may be difficult to simply set aside. But the basis of recovery is learning how you can replace some of the negative qualities within those roles at various times in your relationships. This process of replacement or relearning of old behaviors can improve the quality of your interactions.

Reflection

Think back on past unhealthy relationships. What are some of the effects these relationships have had on you in various areas, such as self-esteem, stress level, or your sense of growth and maturity?

Activity

Now it's time to look at your personal reactions to this chapter. Use your notebook to write your feelings on the following areas.

- Look at the roles played in your relationships. Do you identify with one or more of the roles? In what ways have they been evidenced in your interactions with others?

- Think about the characteristics of the roles. Record the characteristics with which you identify. Are there others you can add that have occurred in your relationships?

PART II

BUILDING HEALTHY RELATIONSHIPS

*Our dilemma is that we hate change, but we love it at the same time.
What we want is for things to remain the same but get better.*
                                            — Sydney J. Harris

CHAPTER THREE

Making Changes

As adult children, we all would probably like to make changes as long as we don't have to put too much effort into it. The fantasizer in us may dream of better relationships; the controller in us may believe that we can certainly make that happen; the dependent person in us may yearn to find the right person who can help us; the isolator in us may desire to change; the nurturer in us may believe that, with care and support, we can affect those changes.

To dream, to yearn, to desire, to care enough, to support ourselves, and to want to make the changes — these are all the elements we need to start to do things in a different way. *But we have to want to make changes badly enough in order for them to be effective.* In reality, most of us are reluctant to make changes unless they're absolutely necessary. Once we decide our unhealthy lives and behaviors are unacceptable, we can work on making them better. The key word in this section is *change.* Margo Adair talks about this in *Working Inside Out: Tools for Change:*

> How often do you find yourself with the same script but with different actors (different friends, or lovers)? If you change your interior environment using new scripts you will free yourself to create *lasting* change around you. *Change must happen both inside and outside.* . . . We are creatures of habit; if we don't *choose* to act differently we simply behave in known familiar ways. But with an act of *will*

35

choose to put yourself on a new stage . . . new actions create new experience.[1]

Later in this book, five elements will be examined that we can use to improve our relationships. Before moving to this section, it's important to become familiar with the Twelve Steps we can use to begin to make changes in our relationships as well as in our lives.

Steps for Changes

Members of Alcoholics Anonymous, Al-Anon, Overeaters Anonymous, and other self-help groups use a Twelve Step program for recovery from the effects of personal, self-defeating characteristics. These Steps help them take an honest look at themselves, become ready to make changes, and develop a sense of spirituality that will help them facilitate such changes.

These same Steps can be used by us to help us improve our interactions with others. The Steps can help us take an honest look at ourselves in our present relationships with others without dwelling on the past. They can help us become ready to make changes and can offer us the means to develop a sense of spirituality that can guide us through our changes.

What follows is a discussion of each of the Twelve Steps with suggestions on how to apply each Step to our process of making changes in relationships. The discussion that follows is based on the Twelve Steps of Alcoholics Anonymous.

Step One
We admitted we were powerless over (alcohol) — that our lives had become unmanageable.
The word *alcohol* can be replaced with whatever behavior we feel we need to change. For example, we might rephrase the Step to read: "I admit that I am powerless over my addiction to people — that my life has become unmanageable because of this addiction."

---

[1] Adair, Margo, *Working Inside Out: Tools for Change*, Wingbow Press, Berkeley, CA, 1984, pp. 212-214.

There are two key words in this Step that we need to understand in our process of change. The first is *powerless*. In terms of our relationships it may mean we feel we are no longer in control — that the area in which we feel change must occur, such as our addiction to people, has become so unbearable or personally defeating that we find we can no longer control it. We may feel that we alone do not have the power to make this area more bearable. We may feel we are repeating our negative relationship behaviors over and over again without knowing how to stop the recurring behavior. We may feel totally helpless to affect any change; hence, we are powerless.

The second word we need to define and understand is *unmanageable*. In terms of our relationships it may mean we feel miserable, unhappy, or lost. It may mean we find it difficult to focus on anything else other than the state of our relationships. It may mean we are dissatisfied with our behaviors in our relationships and find we can't manage these behaviors.

The First Step can help us make changes in our relationships when we are ready to admit there is an unmanageable area that makes us feel powerless. Once we make this admission we are ready to go to Step Two.

Step Two

Came to believe that a Power greater than ourselves could restore us to sanity.

When we admit in Step One that we're powerless, we are also admitting we don't have the capabilities by ourselves to make the changes we feel we need to make. We need help in making those changes.

But where do we go to get help? Although we may be able to talk to a person or people in our lives about the state of our relationships, these people can't necessarily give us the ability to make our relationships more manageable.

So who can we turn to for help? There is no person outside of our lives who can help us, but there is something inside of us to which we can turn. Once we are ready to admit we alone are not capable of making everything better in our relationships we are ready to accept help from a spiritual source. Within us is where a sense of our spirituality resides. That is what the phrase *Power greater than ourselves* means. Some people view this Power as God, a sense of connection to the universe around them, or a sense of faith and trust that we are taken care of. Simply put, belief in a Power greater than ourselves means we accept that we alone do not have the power to make the changes necessary to restore our relationships to a more manageable condition. While this may be a difficult concept to grasp if we've lived our lives up to this point as a controlling person, this Step asks us to let go of some of the control.

We don't have to be "religious," believe in God, go to church, or read religious texts to work with this Step. The importance of this Step lies in its ability to help us make changes when we believe there is something or some being who can assist us. Once we accept the existence of this kind of help, we are ready for Step Three.

Step Three
   Made a decision to turn our will and our lives over to the care of God as we understood Him.

In Step Two we are asked to believe that a Power greater than ourselves exists and can help us make changes. In this Step, we are asked to use this Power and trust that It can help us if we turn our will and lives over to the care of this Power.

We may be able to better understand this Step when we define *will and lives* in terms of our relationships. We may view our will in terms of our desire to manipulate or control others. Or we may see it as the familiar patterns that are strongly entrenched in our personality. Whichever way we define it, will can be seen as the controlling force behind our behavior in relationships.

Our lives can be defined in terms of the state of our relationships — the background we've brought into our relationships, how we interact with others, and how healthy or unhealthy the interactions are.

These two areas — our will and our lives — are what we want to turn over to our Higher Power. Turning them over means we are ready to let go of the things we want to change and receive help in changing them by using our spiritual strength. This will free us to work on identifying particular areas to change. That freedom will allow us to do the soul-searching work in Step Four.

Step Four
Made a searching and fearless moral inventory of ourselves.

In order to improve the quality of our relationships, we need to work on ourselves. It is difficult to love someone else until we first know how to love ourselves. That saying can also be applied to relationships. We can't have healthy relationships unless we are healthy. What we bring into our relationships will ultimately determine the overall state of the relationship. Having a relationship with a healthy person doesn't necessarily mean the relationship is healthy. It takes two healthy people — or two people willing to work on becoming healthier — to improve the relationship.

Our health doesn't only involve our physical state; it also includes our emotional and spiritual state. We may be physically healthy but if we think we're a horrible or inadequate person our emotional health will be low. If we don't have any sense of a Power greater than ourselves our spiritual health will also be low.

To discover the state of our physical, emotional, and spiritual health, we can take an inventory of ourselves. This inventory will explore how we view ourselves in our interactions and see areas that can be changed or improved. This inventory can also reveal areas that are positive in our relationships.

Step Four says the inventory is searching and fearless. This means we need to be honest in our appraisal of ourselves. The only way for us to sort through the confusion, pain, fear, and struggle present in our relationships is to look at ourselves honestly for who we really are. It may be scary for us to take such an honest look at our behavior in our relationships but we can remember to use Steps One, Two, and Three when that fear comes up. We are not alone in this process of self-discovery; we have within us (or are now working on) a sense of spirituality that we can fall back on to give us the courage we need to complete our inventory.

Remember we didn't cause our relationships to be in their present states. We're doing the best we can with the information we were given in our dysfunctional home. That's why we need to take an honest look at ourselves before we learn new information to use to make our relationships happier and healthier.

What follows is a suggested relationship inventory. The areas presented deal specifically with how we feel, act, or react in our interactions with others. Being objective about ourselves is an important part of our inventory.

Members of Twelve Step programs usually begin work on an inventory when they have accumulated some time in their recovery program and feel ready to be as objective as possible about themselves. Before you take your notebook in hand and start answering some of the questions posed in this Step, it's a good idea to first finish reading the entire section discussing the Steps to become familiar with the whole process of making changes in your life. It's also a good idea to read through this Step a few times and think about it before you actually begin to write. Suggestions for completing a Step Four inventory are included in the activity section at the end of this chapter.

Take time now to read through Step Four and the lists that follow to understand how a personal inventory fits into improving your relationships.

Step Four Relationship Inventory
Personal Character Traits, Assets, and Liabilities

Patience With Others. Am I patient with others or do I become unwilling to give them time and space? Do I allow others to do what they need to do for themselves or do I demand constant attention? Do I allow others to make choices for themselves or do I try to control their decisions or actions? Am I patient in my relationships or do I move too quickly and push for what I want?

Open-mindedness Regarding Others. Am I accepting in my attitudes toward others or am I judgmental? Do I allow room for change and growth or do I try to stick with the familiar? Do I accept the differences in others or do I try to make others conform to me?

Courtesy/Kindness Toward Others. Am I kind and courteous toward others, even strangers, or are my actions hurtful? Do I use a smile and kind words or is my expression serious and the tone of my voice harsh? Can I go out of my way to do something nice for another or am I too self-focused?

Expression of Caring. Do I show my feelings of caring toward others or am I afraid to risk such expression of feeling? Do I allow others to show me caring or do I push them away with my actions or words?

Generosity Toward Others. Am I willing to give to others by sharing my time and energy or do I have difficulty giving? Do I listen to others or am I more concerned about the things I need to say? Do I find it's okay to give material things to others or am I possessive of my belongings?

Sharing With Others. Do I let others hear and see what is important to me or am I afraid to share such things with others? Am I willing to try to achieve a balance in give-and- take with others or are the scales tipped in only one direction?

Trusting Others. Do I believe what others tell me or am I suspicious of their words or deeds? Can I accept that some negative feelings are a part of any relationship or am I looking for a perfect relationship? Am I willing to trust those who care for me or am I mistrustful of anyone who would care?

Honesty With Others. Am I willing to be open and honest in my communication with others or do I find myself hiding behind lies and secrets? Is it important that people see me for who I really am or is it better that they believe what I want them to believe?

Forgiveness of Others. Am I willing to forgive the words or deeds of others or do I hold on to hurt, resentment, and anger? Is it easier to treat the differences and disagreements I may have with others with open, honest discussion or with silence and avoidance?

Consistency With Others. Am I easy to be with or do I have inconsistent mood swings? Are my actions and words the same from day to day or do I give mixed messages? Do my actions back up my words?

Willingness to Admit Mistakes. If I am wrong can I admit it or do I make excuses for myself? Can I listen to criticism and suggestions from others about mistakes I may have made or do I choose not to deal with them? Am I willing to forgive myself even if others do not forgive me?

Calmness Around Others. Am I relaxed with others or do I feel fidgety or anxious? Do I let others see the real me when I'm around them or do I put on an act? When there is controversy or difficulty, do I try to work through it or do I retreat into tension and fear?

Expression of Nonsexual Love. Can I do caring and nurturing things for others? Can I tell them I love them? Do I feel it's okay to feel love for co-workers? For my friends? For strangers?

Expression of Sexual Love. Can I do caring and nurturing things for the person with whom I'm intimate? Can I express feelings of love? Do I feel it's okay to share and talk about our sexual expression?

Confidence Around Others. Do I feel comfortable around others or do I isolate? Can I be myself around people or do I put on an act? Am I willing to express my thoughts and feelings or am I afraid not to go along with the crowd?

Sincerity With Others. Do I let people trust me? Am I open and honest with others? Do I feel it's important to express my thoughts and feelings to others? Do my words and actions show I am sincere?

Optimism Around Others. Do I look at the glass as half full or half empty? Can I find the silver lining in the dark cloud? Am I easily defeated or a strong survivor?

Self-Image Around Others. Do I feel good about myself when I'm with others or do I have negative feelings about myself? Is it more important for me to accept myself or for others to accept me?

Fear Around Others. Do I feel insecure or fearful when I'm with others? Am I afraid of what they may think of me? Am I afraid to open up and take risks with people? Is it easier for me to isolate rather than communicate?

Anger. Do I often feel anger toward people or when I'm with them? Is the anger I feel appropriate or am I using anger to distance myself from others or control them? Can I express appropriate anger in ways that are beneficial in my relationships?

Resentments. Do I often feel resentments toward people or when I'm with them? Are my resentments a result of a desire to control others or to place focus on myself?

Self-Pity Around Others. Do I tend to blame others for my faults or difficulties? Do I use negative circumstances in my life for positive results or do I use them to manipulate the feelings of others?

Jealousy Toward Others. Do I give space to those in my life or am I possessive? Do I use negative circumstances in my life for positive results or do I use them to manipulate the feelings of others?

Selfishness With Others. Do I notice my needs rather than the needs of others? Can I give to others without any thought of what they can give in return? Do I have expectations from others or do I accept what they can give to me?

Criticism of Others. Do I judge others harshly? Am I willing to accept the rights of others no matter who they are or what they do?

Outlook Around Others. Is it easier for me to be happy or sad? Do I believe I can let go of negative feelings with others or do I believe, "Misery loves company"?

There are also five basic components to healthy relationships we will discuss in this book: trust, honesty, individuality, nurturing, and knowledge. To make positive changes in our relationships and, ultimately, in ourselves, it's important to learn how to express each of these components in healthy ways. We can begin this process of understanding by exploring what each of these areas means to us as an individual in our relationship with ourselves. Notice that the first letters of each word, when placed together in succession, spell THINK. We can consider the role each component plays in our lives. To do that, define what each component means: what is trust, what is honesty, what is individuality, what is nurturing, and what is knowledge? Then think about how we might use each component in our relationship with ourselves. We can ask ourselves the following questions:

- Trust. Do I trust myself? Do I believe I can do what I set out to do?
- Honesty. Am I honest with myself? Am I aware of my capabilities and abilities, as well as my limitations?
- Individuality. Do I live my life as an individual? Do I make decisions that are right for me?

43

- Nurturing. Do I take care of my physical, emotional, and spiritual health? Can I set limits and balances in my life?
- Knowledge. Am I aware of who I am? Am I growing and maturing through the experiences I have in my life?

We may have an image of what an ideal relationship should be like. Perhaps this image has come from the media, from relationships we have observed, or as a result of the type of relationship we want.

It's important to explore what our image of a relationship is to determine whether our image can realistically be obtained.

We can ask ourselves: What is my image of the ideal relationship? What are the components of this relationship? Is this relationship realistic? Why or why not? Am I looking for fantasy relationships in my life or do I accept relationships for what they are?

After we've completed our inventory, we're ready to work on our Fifth Step.

Step Five
Admitted to God, to ourselves, and to another human being the exact nature of our wrongs.

After taking Step Four, we will probably discover some areas we'd like to improve. Once we complete Step Four we can keep our responses and discoveries to ourselves or we can share this information.

As adult children we may not want to share our revelations with others. We may not want someone else to know our weak points. We may be ashamed at some of our answers and recall feelings of guilt and shame that we felt in our childhood. We may believe that what we discover about ourselves are secrets that shouldn't be shared with another. We may feel that our answers validate any bad feelings we already have about ourselves.

But very little good will come out of Step Four if Step Five isn't used. The purpose of Step Five is to form relationships with those around us by letting them see us for who we really are — the good points as well as the bad. Sharing our Step Four findings with another person validates our findings and lets us share our vulnerable side.

Through this sharing we may find support and caring that can give us the courage to make improvements in our interactions with others.

If we share our inventory with someone we trust we may find we're not alone in some of our thoughts and feelings. We could share our inventory with another adult child who has done some Twelve Step work in his or her own recovery. Select someone who we identify with, who we feel we can trust, and who can help us be objective about ourselves. It may not be a good idea to choose a friend, lover, spouse, or family member.

If we attend adult children meetings, we can share our inventory with our sponsor. We can let our sponsor read our inventory when it's been completed or we can simply talk to our sponsor and together outline some areas where we'd like to make changes. Our sponsor may point out positive areas we haven't recognized in our inventory or may suggest we set more realistic goals. We can listen to the feedback we receive and revise our inventory if necessary.

As we share our inventory it's important to strengthen our spirituality by sharing our findings with our Higher Power. When we wish to make changes or want to ask for forgiveness in some areas, our faith and trust in a Higher Power can help give us courage and patience.

Remember that while our sponsor can give us validation, praise, and advice on our inventory, a spiritual force can give us the strength to carry out the changes we wish to make.

Step Six

Were entirely ready to have God remove all these defects of character.

It may be difficult for us to look back over our inventory and see areas that need work. As adult children we may have spent most of our lives believing we have been wrong in many things. To see some of these on paper and have them referred to as "defects of character" can be disheartening.

We didn't cause those defects of character. It's important to look at the "wrongs" in our inventory as "self-defeating characteristics." That means there are parts of our behavior that aren't helpful to our growth.

Step Six asks us to accept these self-defeating characteristics as temporary parts of our personality. These characteristics can be removed or changed when we're ready and willing to let them go. No person can help us do that. Only our spiritual force and personal motivation can start the wheels of change and self-improvement in motion. Then we're ready for Step Seven.

Step Seven
   Humbly asked Him to remove our shortcomings.
   After we've become ready to let go of our self-defeating characteristics which have held us down and enabled us to continue our negative relationship behaviors, we can begin to let them go. Think of this Step as being very similar to Step One where we admit our interactions with others are unmanageable. In Step Seven, we are admitting we can't get rid of our self-defeating characteristics by ourselves.
   The key word in this section is *humbly*. To be humble in our request to have our negative characteristics removed, we are contacting our inner self and saying, "I don't like these negative characteristics, and I need them to change. But I can't do this alone. I need your help." To be humble means to let go of our controlling or manipulative behaviors. To be humble means to be patient and gentle in our request without setting time limits or constraints. To be humble means to remember there is a Higher Power who is capable of performing things we cannot do alone.

Step Eight
   Made a list of all persons we had harmed, and became willing to make amends to them all.
   Once we've asked our Higher Power for help in removing our self-defeating characteristics we can start to do the direct work to help improve our interactions with others. Some of our shortcomings, liabilities (anger, resentment, jealousy), or behaviors may have affected our relationships in unhealthy ways. We may have caused another person pain, confusion, fear, sadness, or feelings of abandonment because of our self-defeating behaviors.

Step Eight asks us to identify people we may have harmed in the course of our relationships: a friend whose help we rejected, a lover we pushed away through possessiveness and jealousy, or a boss we walked out on in anger. This may also include our parents, who we may have lashed out against at times when they were so impaired by their chemical dependency that they really had no power over their lives and the consequences of their behavior. Nevertheless, this Step does not ask us to identify people who may have harmed us, such as our parents. The focus should be kept entirely on our actions with others.

Make a list of these people and become willing to make amends to them. Once we become willing, we're ready for Step Nine.

Step Nine
Made direct amends to such people wherever possible, except when to do so would injure them or others.

Step Nine suggests we make our amends to the people we considered in Step Eight but only if such amends will not cause them further harm or pain. Think about whether or not our amends will cause renewed grief, anger, or pain. Don't try to make amends if we're still holding on to resentments, jealousy, or anger because it may be hard to be sincere.

When we make an amend, it's important not to fall into the trap of making excuses or assigning blame for our behaviors. Our childhood cannot be used as an excuse when we're making an amend. "I'm sorry I beat you. My father used to do the same thing to me," or, "I'm sorry I pushed you away from me whenever you tried to get close. That's the way my mother showed love." These are not amends, but defenses of our behavior.

Step Ten
Continued to take personal inventory and when we were wrong promptly admitted it.

Our inventory should be viewed as ongoing. It's important for us to reexamine our inventory often because our self-defeating characteristics may be so deeply ingrained. Familiar but negative behaviors can occur anytime we feel adult children's issues coming up. We may not be able to prevent those feelings and may find it difficult not to fall back on our past coping mechanisms when we become threatened or uneasy.

It's important that we continue to make amends when we recognize wrongs we have committed. The key word in this Step is *promptly*. For some of us, that can be days, weeks, or even months. Self-defeating behaviors can become so much a part of our personality that it may be hard to recognize when a behavior is occurring. But as we change, we may find our amends-making times become shorter and shorter. That's a good sign because it means our inventory has put us in touch with our actions and behaviors so we can make changes necessary to our growth in relationships.

Step Eleven
Sought through prayer and meditation to improve our conscious contact with God as we understood Him, *praying only for knowledge of His will for us and the power to carry that out.*

While we may want the quality of our relationships to get better right away, remember that we can't do everything at once, nor can we make all the changes ourselves.

The interactions we have with our spiritual power are important to the strength and longevity of the changes we make in our interactions with others. To develop our spirituality we can use prayer and meditation. These tools will help us make conscious contact with our Higher Power.

It's been said that prayer is talking to our Higher Power and meditation is listening to It. When we pray we can ask for help from our Higher Power to improve our relationships with others. When we meditate we can visualize positive and healthy relationships in our lives. We can also use music or guided meditations, or interesting activities. We can physically relax, or we can sit quietly for a short time. We can let our minds relax and become willing to let desired changes happen.

Step Twelve

Having had a spiritual awakening as a result of these steps, we tried to carry this message to (alcoholics), and to practice these principles in all our affairs.

This is the last of the dozen Steps for change. Whether viewed alone or as a "wrap up" to the knowledge gained in the eleven Steps that precede it, Step Twelve can be a powerful catalyst for change.

First, what is a spiritual awakening? Think back to Step Two which suggested that we may need to ask for help in order to make important changes in our lives. Remember Step Three which asked us to consider our relationship with God, as we understand that God. A spiritual awakening is the opening up of the channels of contact between ourselves and the God of our understanding, whether we understand God in a religious sense, define It as a Higher Power, or see It as a spiritual or ethereal symbol.

We may have difficulty accepting the concept of a Power greater than ourselves at this point in our lives. That's okay. Many of us grew up questioning the existence of a God because of the circumstances and emotions in our childhoods. We may reach adulthood with little or no acceptance of a God. But today, we can remember this Step refers to a spiritual *awakening*. Our awakening can be seen as a gradual growing awareness — one that can clarify itself over time.

The second part of this Step suggests that we carry the message of the Steps to others. As we begin to make changes and improvements in our relationships with others through the Steps, our awareness of more positive ways of interacting with others can increase. This ever-growing awareness can be seen not only as a valuable resource for us, but also for others who may be struggling in their relationships. Asking for help, as well as offering it, are important components in recovery from unhealthy behaviors. Step Twelve recommends that as we improve the quality of our relationships, we can carry our positive growth to others by speaking at meetings and being a sponsor to another adult child.

The third and final component of Step Twelve is applying what we've learned from each of the Steps to the experiences in our daily lives. As an adult child, we need to keep in mind how easy it is for us to fall back into negative behavior patterns because the positive behavior patterns may be relatively new for us. Because of this, it's important to keep in mind — as much as possible — the positive message of recovery and growth that each of the Steps offers. Some people like to set aside daily meditation or prayer time to keep the channels of communication open between themselves and their spiritual Power. Others like to carry an inspirational book or pamphlet with them to refer to during difficult times. Many gain strength from the spirit of fellowship and use the telephone or meetings to keep on the positive track.

But whatever method we use, we can remember to strive for a balance between our emotional sides and our spiritual sides as we work toward making changes in our relationships. We can be gentle with ourselves. We can be patient. Positive changes can happen without a daily struggle. All we have to do is make ourselves ready and willing to change. Remember, the journey of a thousand miles begins with one step.

A Final Note on the Steps

The Twelve Steps of Alcoholics Anonymous are currently in use in many Twelve Step programs because they are valuable tools in the process of recovery.

As adult children, some of us may have difficulty with the Twelve Steps because of particular words used. Since all of us do not come from alcoholic homes, Step One's reference to alcohol can be seen as an exclusion by those of us who were sexually abused or came from homes where there was chronic illness, gambling, or other dysfunction. In those cases, we can substitute words of our own to capture our sense of powerlessness and unmanageability in our lives. Step One could be revised to reflect, "I am powerless over my mother's cancer," or, "I am powerless over the sexual abuse of the past."

In addition, we may have strong feelings about the Step Six reference to "defects of character" or the Step Seven reference to "shortcomings." Many of us in recovery prefer to say we suffer from self-defeating characteristics.

Finally, some of us see Steps Eight and Nine as suggestions to apologize or make amends to parents who abused us physically or emotionally. In recovery, we may want to treat these Steps as tools to use in our daily lives or with relationships outside the dysfunctional childhood home.

Summary

The Twelve Steps of recovery can be used by adult children who wish to work through relationship issues and improve the quality of their interactions with others. The message of each Step, combined with the introspective inventory work in Step Four, can help you begin the process of identification of your self-defeating characteristics in order to make changes and improvements in your relationships with others.

Reflection

Now that you've read through each of the Steps, what are some of your initial impressions about them? How do you feel you can grow from your work with them? In what ways do you feel they can help you improve the quality of your interactions with others?

Activity

Now it's time to take a Fourth Step inventory. Use your notebook to write down your thoughts on the following areas. When you do your inventory, be sure you're not feeling in a low mood; otherwise, your responses will likely be negative or harsh. Also, it's a good idea to complete as much as you can in one sitting, without interruption.

Personal Character Traits

Write a few sentences in regard to the character traits that you especially identified with in the Step Four Relationship Inventory. How has the trait been evidenced in past relationships? In what way — positive or negative — is it present in your relationships today? Try to answer the questions, assesss whether you'd like to improve or change your behaviors, and identify how you'd like to make those changes. Try to be specific. Don't say, "I want to be more patient with everybody and tomorrow I will be." It's more helpful to say, "I'd like to be more patient in my interactions with my boss. To do so, I will pause before I speak to him and not interrupt when he's talking."

Identify personal qualities that you bring into a relationship that benefit it. In what ways are those qualities positive?

Relationship Components

Write a few sentences about how you've handled each of the five relationship components in your relationships by giving one specific example for each question.

Trust. When were you trusting in a relationship? When weren't you trusting in a relationship?

Honesty. When were you honest in a relationship? When weren't you honest in a relationship?

Individuality. When did you feel like an individual in a relationship? When didn't you feel like an individual in a relationship?

Nurturing. When did you nurture in a relationship? When didn't you nurture in a relationship?

Knowledge. When did you use knowledge in a relationship? When didn't you use knowledge in a relationship?

Relationship Images

Answer the following questions:

- Write about your image of a perfect relationship, be it with a boss or co-worker, spouse, friend, or long-term relationship. Give details about it.
- Look at the description of your perfect relationship. How have your actual relationships lived up to or fallen short of this image? Give details.
- Reflect on your answers to one and two. Try to find a balance between your image of perfection and the reality of actual relationships. Now write about how you think you can improve the quality of your relationships and achieve this balance.
- Can you accept the fact that no relationship you have will ever be perfect? Explain your answer.

CHAPTER FOUR

Elements of Healthy Relationships

To bring about positive changes in ourselves, the Steps will be useful time and time again. The changes we make through the help of the Steps can ultimately affect the quality of our relationships. The healthier we become, the healthier our relationships can become.

To bring about positive changes in our relationships, we need to learn how to work with the components that directly affect the quality of our interactions with others. One word can help us learn and remember all we need to know about relationships: THINK. That word can be seen as an acronym for the five components of a healthy relationship which were examined in the Step Four inventory: Trust, Honesty, Individuality, Nurturing, and Knowledge.

Working through an understanding of these five areas and using exercises to help us initiate positive changes in those areas are the goals for building healthy relationships.

One further word from Margo Adair will be helpful before we begin learning how to incorporate changes.

> If you find yourself sliding back into old patterns, don't interpret it as a sign of failure; quite to the contrary, if you weren't changing you wouldn't notice the backslide. . . . In the past you took that behavior for granted and didn't see it. Give yourself a break, be patient with yourself — it all takes time. Whenever you discover yourself in old patterns just fo-

cus on the new patterns and choose to act out of their power.[2]

Trust

The first and most important component of any healthy relationship is trust. Even if we have the four other components in our relationships, they won't be strong and positive without the development of a certain level of trust.

Trust can be seen as a basis of belief, faith, and confident reliance on someone's character, honesty, or strength. In relationships, trust usually comes from two areas: trust in self and trust in others. We must first trust ourselves before we can trust someone else. For example, do we trust that we won't hurt another person in a relationship? That we want to do our best to try to make changes? That we will try to make a relationship work?

Without trust in ourselves, we will probably have difficulty trusting others *consistently*. As adult children, consistency is an especially important word for those of us who tend to either trust anyone and everyone with all the details of our lives or trust no one with no detail of our lives. We may have difficulty finding a real balance.

Without trust in a relationship there will be little or no basis for faith or confidence in the relationship itself. When this happens, unhealthy behaviors can begin to grow.

Unhealthy Trust

Untrustworthy relationships for us probably began in the childhood home. One or both parents may have made promises to us that were rarely kept. They may have said they were interested in us but rarely or never attended any of our school or athletic functions. They may have told us they loved us at inappropriate times or in inappropriate ways. They may have sporadically attended meals or family activities or may have ruined holiday gatherings from time to time. Because of all the inconsistencies in our early lives, we may have

---

[2]Adair, Margo, *Working Inside Out: Tools for Change*, Wingbow Press, Berkeley, CA, 1984, pp. 212-214.

learned to not trust what was said or shown to us.

The first time we trusted someone outside of our home and were let down may have been devastating for us. The let down could have been about something minor, like having someone cancel a plan, or something major, like telling an intimate secret to a friend and then hearing our secret shared with others.

Whether the incident was minor or major didn't matter to us because we felt we had learned one thing: not only could our parents not be trusted, but people outside the home could not be trusted either. Over time we may have learned not to depend on people but to rely solely on ourselves.

But then we may have found we couldn't even trust ourselves. We may have become involved with people who didn't treat us well. Even though we were unhappy with them we couldn't seem to break away from them. We may have felt we were constantly setting ourselves up with people who were insensitive, unkind, uncaring — maybe even physically or verbally abusive to us. We'd tell ourselves we deserved better but couldn't figure out how to find it. We may have even joked about our radar for finding unhealthy people. This joking may have masked the lack of faith we had in our ability to stay away from unkind people.

Without knowing where to turn for trust in our lives, we may have used chemicals, food, charge cards, or other addictive substances to soothe our loneliness. The feelings these material things gave us may have been easy to trust at first, but after awhile the pleasure may have changed to discomfort. Once we began our addictive cycle, what little trust we had in ourselves may have dissolved. Once trust has been lost it becomes harder to reestablish trusting feelings. No relationship can survive for very long without some degree of healthy trust.

Healthy Trust

To form healthy relationships we first need to reestablish trust in our lives. One of the first places to begin to build trust is with ourselves, because we can then take a basis of faith into a relationship with another.

55

How do we learn to trust ourselves? We must begin with *acceptance* of who we are right now. Looking at our Step Four inventory, we can see our assets and shortcomings and start making the changes and improvements we determined from our inventory. We don't have to change completely or perfectly and can do it at our own pace.

Our spirituality can also help us to develop trust in ourselves. By having faith in our Higher Power and accepting that this Power is watching over us, we may find it easier to trust we are doing okay. We can allow ourselves plenty of time and space to rebuild trust in ourselves.

Trust-Building Exercises

When you wake up, set one goal that will be easy to achieve and will help you feel good about yourself. For example, "I'll have an enjoyable ride to and from work today and not lose my temper in rush-hour traffic."

Keep a journal to record details of any daily happening in which you were proud of your behavior or actions. For example, "Today my boss corrected a report I had written. I was really happy with myself when I didn't overreact to her criticism."

Before going to bed think of at least five things you like about yourself. They can be simple statements such as "I'm a good cook," or a more complex one such as "I think I'm doing a really good job in improving my attitude toward my ex-husband."

Over time we may begin to notice we are consistently giving ourselves praise in certain areas. This consistency can help build a feeling of trust in ourselves, which we can bring into our relationships.

Trusting Others

After we begin to trust ourselves, we're in a much better position to trust others. But trust isn't something given equally to everyone we meet, under any circumstance. Trust is a gradual building process where we learn who and when to trust. We need to look at others for who they are, what they do, and how they act. That recognition will help us determine the level of trust we can have for individuals.

*   *   *

Cathy started a new job as manager of five people in a company. One of her first tasks was to select an assistant. Cathy knew nothing about any of the employees except what was in their files. She observed them for a period of a month: their timeliness, work habits, interactions with others, and how they handled problems that arose in the course of a work day.

By the third week she was able to see that Carl seemed to distinguish himself above the others. He was always on time for work and always met his deadlines. Cathy knew she had to have an assistant she could depend on and Carl displayed this consistency for her.

*   *   *

Cathy developed a level of trust in Carl from his actions. We can do the same thing by observing others' actions. The spouse who never forgets our birthday, the friend who always phones when she'll be late, and the lover who shows up on time for dates can all be trusted because of their consistency. Consistency is the key to building trust.

As long as the people we're involved with in our relationships are consistent, our level of trust in them can grow. But if we're given mixed messages or their behavior is inconsistent, our trust can be on shaky ground.

*   *   *

Phil and Marsha have been dating for six months. Right from the start Phil said he didn't want a commitment from Marsha. So when Marsha was asked out by Gene she accepted. When Phil heard about this he became very angry and told her he didn't want her dating other men.

Naturally Marsha was confused. Which message did she trust from Phil — that he didn't want to be committed or that he wanted her to date only him?

*   *   *

Similarly, if we're giving mixed messages to others in our relationships, we're not helping to build a strong foundation of trust. To build trusting relationships we must be patient and give ourselves and the other person the opportunity to make mistakes and rectify them. To return to the example of Phil and Marsha, they need to sit down and talk about what each other wants from the relationship. Phil may say he wants to try a committed relationship for a few weeks. At the end of the three weeks, he may decide he wants to return to the "open" relationship. That doesn't mean Marsha can no longer trust him whenever he expresses his feelings about what he wants from their relationship. It means they need to keep talking about their feelings in the relationship. What Marsha can trust is that she and Phil are interested in each other and care enough to want to work on their relationship. The relationship needs time and patience.

A healthy, trusting relationship usually has the following qualities:

- belief in some level of commitment to the relationship;
- faith that any problems will be discussed;
- concern for the welfare of each other as well as for the relationship;
- clarity about the status of the relationship and the feelings involved.

Each of these components of a healthy, trusting relationship is also based on honesty.

Honesty

There are three definitions that can be used to discover what honesty means. The first is *telling the truth*. That's probably the most basic and well-known of all the definitions. The second is *acknowledging the truth*. If we get angry when someone lies to us, then being honest means we can admit and *accept* our anger. The third definition is *dealing in the truth*. This involves communication to verbalize the truth. For example we can say, "I feel angry when you lie to me. I would prefer you tell me the truth."

Unhealthy Honesty

Our childhood home was probably a haven for dishonesty. This dishonesty may have hidden many truths in our family. We may have often heard, "Of course I'm fine," "Your father's tired and needs to rest," or "I promise I'll never do that again." We know now those were lies, but at the time we heard them we may have accepted them as the truth.

We probably grew up learning to accept dishonest excuses, half truths, and lies as normal. We may have even begun telling lies, discovering it was easier to hide behind a lie than it was to tell the truth.

In adulthood we may have experienced the same dishonesty in our relationships. We may have lied to customers and co-workers to cover for our alcoholic boss. We may have denied the affairs we knew our spouse was having. We may have used lies to break plans with friends or to take time off from work. After so many years of lying we may have become more comfortable with the untruths. But over time the dishonesty may have taken its toll. We may no longer be in touch with our feelings nor able to verbalize them. New relationships may be based on dishonesty rather than honesty.

We can also remember that we don't have to tell a lie in order to practice dishonesty through denial. If we close our eyes to family and relationship problems, and allow ourselves and others to be swept along in negative circumstances, then we are being dishonest. The silence of not acknowledging painful events and behaviors may be a conspiracy of dishonesty for many of us.

Healthy Honesty

Healthy honesty begins by taking an honest look at ourselves and the limitations we may bring into a relationship. As in exploring trust, our Step Four inventory can be used to give us insights. For example, we may honestly know we aren't capable of being in a committed relationship right now. If we ignore this and try to be in one, we are being dishonest both with ourselves and our partner. Similarly, if we have a difficult time being around people who are outgoing and energetic, we're lying to ourselves if we choose to be friends with them.

Healthy honesty involves communication with ourselves as well as with others. But communication with the self always comes first. We can't be honest with others if we aren't honest with ourselves. Self-communication begins by acknowledging our feelings without making excuses for them. It means admitting our shortcomings, wrongs, and difficulties.

Self-communication also involves acknowledging our feelings without making excuses for someone else. It means admitting our feelings when others have affected us. For example, if we feel anger when our lover shows up late for dinner without calling, we're being dishonest if we discredit our anger with excuses like: "The office was probably busy," "Traffic may have been bad," or "I shouldn't feel anger because that will just start an argument." We have a right to our feelings; we wouldn't have them if they weren't meant to be there. We can acknowledge and accept them as part of being honest with ourselves.

Once we're honest with ourselves, we'll be able to be more honest with others. This happens by communication. The key to honesty in relationships is open, honest communication.

Being Honest With Others

The key to communicating honestly with others is to keep the focus on ourselves. Speak in terms of ourselves and how we feel without judging others' actions or behaviors. We can say, "I feel . . . ," not "You did. . . ." That way, the other person will focus on how we feel about an action or behavior he or she did. It is then up to that person to take responsibility to decide whether or not to change that action or behavior in the future. For example, we can say to our tardy lover: "I'm angry you're late. I would have appreciated a phone call." This communication of honest feelings is important.

Remember, too, that healthy communication involves *good feelings*. If our lover calls us next time he or she will be late, we can share positive feelings, "I'm really glad you called to let me know you'll be late. Thanks!" This gives the other person a chance to know what pleases us.

Sometimes, however, communication of honest feelings may not be beneficial. We may honestly feel a friend has gained a lot of weight and looks terrible. We can acknowledge that feeling to ourselves, but saying something may only cause hurt and damage a good relationship. The key phrase in communicating honest feelings to another is *only if it is necessary*. If it will improve our interactions and help develop a better understanding of each other, then communication is probably necessary.

A healthy, honest relationship usually has the following qualities:

- verbal sharing of feelings, both good and bad;
- acceptance of all shared feelings;
- discussion of items of importance;
- honesty in words as well as actions.

There's a lot more that can be learned about healthy communication. College courses, therapy, self-help books, and seminars can all be helpful in developing effective communication skills between the individuals involved in the relationship.

Individuality

Individuality means having a sense of self. This sense of self is composed of things that give us personal definition — likes and dislikes, needs and wants, goals and desires, skills and abilities, limits and boundaries. Without a sense of self we may not be able to be an individual within a relationship. We may instead be dependent on someone else to give us a sense of self.

Lack of Individuality

Very rarely in the dysfunctional home were we allowed to be our own person. If we were brought up in a controlling or rigid environment we were probably given very little freedom to be ourselves. If we were brought up in a neglectful or an abusive environment we may have learned being ourselves caused problems. In our

61

home, family members with problems may have received attention while those of us with motivation, individuality, and self-caring were ignored.

Over time we may have learned it was best to blend in by looking, acting, and being like other people. We may have learned to be a great imitator of those we liked in order to gain their attention and affection. We may have taken on the dreams of others, believing they were what we wanted too. We may have chosen to do what others wanted to do to keep from being different. We may have agreed with what others said in order to make interactions easier. We may not have become an individual by developing our sense of self; instead we may have become what we thought others wanted us to be.

Healthy Individuality

We don't have to know everything about ourselves to be healthy or to be involved in healthy relationships. All we need is the desire to get to know the parts of ourselves that have been ignored or suppressed all these years. We can then see ourselves as individuals who have a particular set of personal needs, desires, feelings, and values. We can then apply what we've learned to relate our feelings, needs, and limits to others so they can see us as individuals.

How do we get in touch with ourselves? First, remember that we won't find out everything we need to know about ourselves the minute we make our decision to become our own person. We can take our time and take each day as an exciting experience. We can make up our minds to learn something new about ourselves. Our Step Four inventory can be seen as our first move in getting to know ourselves. As we keep in touch with ourselves beyond the scope of our Step Four inventory, we may discover more things about ourselves.

Individuality With Others

Chances are we may have formed relationships with people who were domineering and controlling. We may still choose to be around such people, but now we need to be aware of how we act so our individuality doesn't get squashed. It's important for us to stand up to controlling people and be clear with them that we have a right to express our feelings and opinions — and to have them respected. The key to healthy individuality in a relationship is to be ourselves.

Not everyone will like this new individual especially if we've been a chameleon who has adapted to make everyone happy. We may hear comments like: "You've changed. I don't think I like this new person." In fact, we may lose some people from our lives. Remember, we are not becoming a new person, we are becoming *our own person*. We are simply recognizing and giving voice to who we have been all along. The healthy relationships in our lives will include acceptance of our newfound individuality and expression. People who are involved in unhealthy relationships with us will most likely feel threatened and may leave us.

It's vital for us to bring a sense of self into our relationships. Relationships are made up of two individuals brought together by one or more commonalities.

A healthy relationship usually has the following qualities:

- acceptance of one another's good and bad qualities;
- no dominance or control of another to change behaviors;
- time to spend apart from one another;
- interest in items of importance to one another.

Once the people in a relationship accept each other for who they are as individuals, nurturing of one another becomes easier.

Nurturing
Nurturing in a healthy relationship means *taking* care of ourselves and *giving* care to another. The taking and giving need to be kept in balance to ensure each person maintains a sense of self yet gives time and attention to the other person.

Unhealthy Nurturing
As a child we needed time, attention, love, and care from our parents, but they probably couldn't give us those things. Even though we may have been told we were loved we might not remember being hugged or held. Even though we may have been told the family was

63

important we might not remember times when our family spent quality time together. Even though we may have been told we were important we might only remember being lonely, hoping someone would notice us.

We may have learned not to make demands on our parents, because they wouldn't be there. Over time we may have chosen to deny we had any needs. We may have desperately searched for someone who could give us all the love and care our parents couldn't give. Yet we may have formed attractions to people who were relatively unavailable to us — repeating the circumstances we had with our parents. Rather than recognize this unavailability and back away from the relationship, we may have struggled day after day in an unhealthy relationship. Our hope was that some day we would be given all the nurturing we needed.

Healthy Nurturing

When we take care of ourselves in a relationship we learn to recognize our needs and give them attention. This is not done for someone else but for ourselves — because we need to. Maybe we've been working late every night of the week. To nurture ourselves, we first need to recognize how we feel. Then we can determine what we need. Once we determine our feelings and our needs we can come up with some choices of things we can do that will help us take care of our need to rest and relax. We can go to bed early. Or we can watch television without making in-depth conversation.

Nurturing ourselves is almost like creating a beautiful flower garden. In order to ensure that each delicate flower is bright and long-lasting we must provide proper nutrition, water, and care. That involves commitment, time, and patience. We can give the same care to ourselves. We are just as delicate and our needs are just as important.

Nurturing Ourselves With Others

Healthy nurturing isn't selfish even though it sometimes means placing our needs ahead of others. For example, if we have planned to spend time with a friend but find we're exhausted on that night, we may need to cancel. Nurturing means we need to take care of ourselves first. Our friend may be disappointed, hurt, or even angry, but part of nurturing ourselves is learning to listen to our limits before we get run down, depressed, stressed out, or unhappy. It's up to us to recognize our needs and communicate them. We're the only ones who can. The key to healthy nurturing in a relationship is understanding how to first nurture ourselves.

But by the same token, the other person in our relationship has a particular set of needs that he or she needs to recognize and communicate. Healthy relationships involve nurturing others when it's possible to do so. A friend may need to talk, a co-worker may need a ride to work while a car is being serviced, or a lover may need to spend time alone. Can we accept this and not demand that he or she change his or her mind? To nurture others means to accept their needs as important and to give care when we can.

A healthy, nurturing relationship has the following qualities:

- kindness and courtesy;
- tenderness and warmth;
- calmness and serenity;
- balance of giving and receiving.

With an understanding of how to nurture one another in a relationship comes the knowledge of how to take care of oneself, as well as another.

Knowledge
This final component of healthy relationships encompasses the material discussed earlier. Knowledge allows us to make mature decisions regarding a relationship. This information is based on realities, not fantasies; facts, not hopes; individuality, not dependency; limitations, not lack of boundaries; change and growth, not stagnation. Knowledge allows us to answer many important questions about a relationship: Is it healthy? Can it grow? Is the other person capable of trust, honesty, individuality, and nurturing? Am I accepted for who I am in the relationship? Are my needs respected? Are we growing to-

gether? Are we making healthy changes for ourselves and for the relationship?

Lack of Knowledge

If we do not know who we are and what we want, we enter relationships without all of the knowledge we need to make them healthy. This lack of knowledge was probably bred in our childhood home where we may have had few role models who knew who they were, what they wanted, and how to get it. One or both of our parents may have been directionless, talking about dreams and desires but never putting them into action. Or we may have had a workaholic parent who was driven about anything job-related but lacked a sense of self away from work.

The information we were given was most likely based on negative messages: don't trust, don't talk, don't feel. If we did meet someone who had healthy behavior, we may have avoided them or may have felt very uncomfortable around them. Instead we may have gravitated toward others who had the same unhealthy relationship behaviors we learned at home.

In order to start learning more about ourselves we can start attending a support group and possibly seek professional counseling on an individual basis. These approaches can help us start building a stronger sense of identity and could reveal just how much we really do know about our needs and desires.

Healthy Knowledge

To be comfortable in healthy relationships we may have to reprogram our way of thinking about relationships. The familiar may not necessarily be healthy, so we may have to work with the unfamiliar until we get used to it. Working with the unfamiliar means developing the four components previously discussed: trust, honesty, individuality, and nurturing. The wisdom we gain from this work will eventually help us make wiser decisions for ourselves and our relationships. The key to healthy knowledge about relationships is putting this knowledge to use.

Healthy Knowledge With Others

It's important to focus on the realities in our relationships. These realities are based on truths that will give us an idea of another person's state of health and how healthy a relationship would be with him or her.

We may see some unhealthy behavior patterns exhibited in our relationships: a dependency or addiction, a lack of trust, an inability to talk honestly about feelings, or an undeveloped sense of self. As we begin to change our unhealthy patterns we'll become more adept at recognizing those behaviors in others. We don't necessarily have to avoid people with these characteristics, but we can be cautious about our interactions with them.

Healthy relationships usually have the following qualities:

- a high level of trust and faith in each other and in the relationship;
- an honest, open communication and sharing;
- a strong sense of individuality and healthy independence;
- a balance in nurturing give and take;
- resolution of issues in the relationship;
- a mature outlook regarding the relationship;
- an ability to recognize unhealthy behaviors;
- an ability to make choices;
- a greater level of tolerance.

Summary

The five components of healthy relationships — Trust, Honesty, Individuality, Nurturing, and Knowledge — need to be understood and developed in order to build growing, maturing relationships. Armed with this knowledge we have the blueprints for building strong foundations in our interactions with others.

Reflection

Take a moment now to look back to your Reflection and Activity comments on Chapter Two of this book. Do you feel differently now about your understanding of healthy relationships? Do you believe the messages and influences of the past can be changed in the present? What are some of the tools you can use to affect such changes?

Activity

Now it's time to examine your personal reactions to this chapter. Use your notebook to write down responses to the following:

Trust-Building Exercise. Take time now to start recording your "daily positive strokes." What are five good qualities you like about yourself? After you do this for two weeks increase the list to ten.

Honesty-Building Exercise. Record "personal myths" — untruths about yourself which you've believed for many years, such as: "I'll never amount to anything." Next to each myth, record the person who may have led you to believe the statement — a family member, boss, or even yourself. Underneath each myth write a positive truth about yourself that disproves the myth: "I'll never have a long-term relationship." (Me!) Truth: "I can have a long-term relationship because I'm learning more about healthy relationships."

Individuality-Building Exercise. Record some of the ways in which you're different from the people with whom you have relationships. For example, "I'm a special needs teacher and no one in my family is," or, "I have a birthmark on my right arm," or, "I'm the only person in the office who knows how to run the photo reduction machine."

Nurturing Exercise. Record at least three physical, emotional, and spiritual needs you have. Then respond to those needs by identifying how you satisfy them or need to satisfy them.

Knowledge-Building Exercise. Based on what you've learned from this book, respond with a few sentences about your reactions to the three unhealthy statements you may have learned in your dysfunctional home: don't talk, don't trust, don't feel.

CHAPTER FIVE

Future Relationships

If we use the components of THINK in our relationships we will probably have a much better chance in forming healthier relationships. But don't use THINK with the expectation that healthy relationships will automatically happen for us. We need to focus on ourselves first, working on ourselves and our needs. We must become healthier *before* our relationships can. The state of a relationship's health is dependent upon the state of health of the people involved in the relationship.

To ensure healthy growth in ourselves and our relationships, we can set our sights on a healthy course.

Setting a Healthy Course

The Step Four inventory can be seen as a whole new beginning for us. The work that we've begun in those few short pages can make all the difference in the world in how we feel about ourselves. We can continue this wonderful work and apply the knowledge we've gained by making a conscious decision to improve our self-esteem. Start to do the things we'd like to do for ourselves without thinking about how others will view them or how they'll benefit our relationships. Remember that any work we do on ourselves will ultimately improve interactions we have with others.

Relationship Affirmations

Many people use positive statements called affirmations to help them have a more positive outlook. Affirmations can be an inspiration for changing negative beliefs.

Affirmations are most effective when we meditate or when our mind is free from the clutter and chaos of the day. For example, don't wait until we're in the middle of an argument with our spouse to say the affirmation, "I am free from anger in my interactions with others." We can start our day — or even our week — with that one simple statement. We can reaffirm the statement every time we have a free moment. After awhile, we'll start to believe we can be free from anger in our interactions with others.

To continue the positive work we've begun in improving ourselves and the quality of our relationships, we can use the following list of affirmative statements to help us develop positive feelings inside. Focus on one affirmation at a time and use it for awhile. After a few days, we can ask ourselves if we've started to feel the positive sentiment expressed in the statement.

If we can't find a relationship affirmation that applies to us from the following list, we can write our own. Be sure to emphasize positive phrasing, such as "I am happy with who I am," rather than "I won't be unhappy with myself."

The following list of affirmations can be helpful in changing our attitudes from negative to positive.

- I am free from insecurities in all my relationships.
- I am free from doubt in all my relationships.
- I am free from fear in all my relationships.
- I like the new person I am becoming.
- I have many good things to share with others.
- I am beautiful and lovable.
- I can be trustworthy in my relationships.
- I can love someone else.
- I can trust _____ in my relationship.
- I am open and honest with myself and with others.
- I can communicate my feelings to others.

- I can accept _____ as an individual.
- I appreciate my qualities and those of the people around me.
- I can be myself and be with others.
- I can let others see who I really am.
- I want good and healthy people all around me.
- I bring good qualities into a relationship.
- I can let others give love and care to me.
- I am blessed by wonderful relationships.

As we grow healthier we will probably find ourselves in the company of healthier people. Our unhealthy relationships may not last as long; our healthier ones may last longer. Over time, we may see ourselves as a different person. Others may see the changes and remark on how good we look. We may start to notice we're living our lives with new patterns of behavior: smiles instead of tears, confidence instead of fears, independence rather than dependence, hope rather than despair.

That means we're on our way to becoming a person who is healthy, whole, and ready for healthy relationships. Congratulations!

THE TWELVE STEPS OF ALCOHOLICS ANONYMOUS*

1. We admitted we were powerless over alcohol — that our lives had become unmanageable.
2. Came to believe that a Power greater than ourselves could restore us to sanity.
3. Made a decision to turn our will and our lives over to the care of God *as we understood Him.*
4. Made a searching and fearless moral inventory of ourselves.
5. Admitted to God, to ourselves, and to another human being the exact nature of our wrongs.
6. Were entirely ready to have God remove all these defects of character.
7. Humbly asked Him to remove our shortcomings.
8. Made a list of all persons we had harmed, and became willing to make amends to them all.
9. Made direct amends to such people wherever possible, except when to do so would injure them or others.
10. Continued to take personal inventory and when we were wrong promptly admitted it.
11. Sought through prayer and meditation to improve our conscious contact with God *as we understood Him,* praying only for knowledge of His will for us and the power to carry that out.
12. Having had a spiritual awakening as a result of these steps, we tried to carry this message to alcoholics, and to practice these principles in all our affairs.

---

*The Twelve Steps are taken from *Alcoholics Anonymous* (Third Edition), published by A.A. World Services, New York, NY., pp. 59-60. Reprinted with permission.

Other titles that will interest you . . .

Once Upon a Time
by Amy E. Dean

For those of us raised in an alcoholic home, Once Upon a Time shows us that there can be a "happily ever after" to our lives. Here, twenty adult children share their stories, revealing the problems they needed to overcome in order to find a bright future filled with freedom from their past. (165 pp.)
Order No. 5010

Days of Healing, Days of Joy
Daily Meditations for Adult Children
by Earnie Larsen and Carol Larsen Hegarty

Spontaneity, openness, trust and playfulness — these are the joys of a carefree childhood that we recovering adult children can capture today with this long-awaited collection of daily meditations.
Order No. 5024

Letting Go of the Need to Control
by Ann M.

An adult child shares how letting go of her controlling behavior has improved her life. The author uses her own experiences to illustrate what controlling behavior is and why those of us raised in alcoholic or other dysfunctional families adopt these patterns and carry them into adulthood. (24 pp)
Order No. 5322

**For price and order information please call one of our
Customer Service Representatives.**

HAZELDEN EDUCATIONAL MATERIALS

(800) 328-9000	(800) 257-0070	(612) 257-4010
(Toll Free U.S. Only)	(Toll Free MN Only)	(AK and Outside U.S.)

Pleasant Valley Road • Box 176 • Center City, MN 55012-0176

First published January, 1988.

Copyright ©1988, Hazelden Foundation.
All rights reserved. No portion of this publication
may be reproduced in any manner without the written
permission of the publisher.

Library of Congress Catalog Card Number: 87-61513

ISBN: 0-89486-460-2

Printed in the United States of America.

MAKING CHANGES:
How Adult Children Can Have Healthier, Happier Relationships

Amy E. Dean